UNDERSTANDING DISEASE AND WELLNESS

Kids' Guides to Why People Get
Sick and How They Can Stay Well

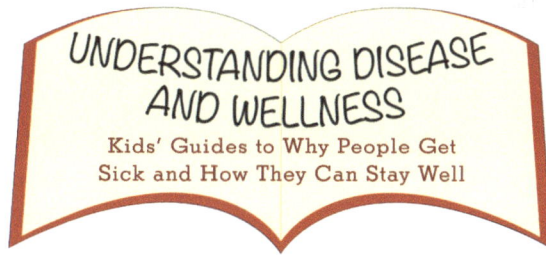

A KID'S GUIDE TO A HEALTHIER YOU

VILLAGE EARTH PRESS

Series List

UNDERSTANDING DISEASE
AND WELLNESS
Kids' Guides to Why People Get
Sick and How They Can Stay Well

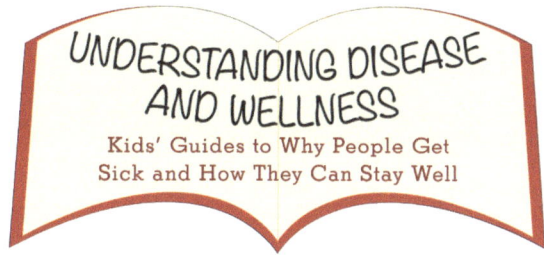

A KID'S GUIDE TO
A HEALTHIER YOU

C. F. Earl

Understanding Disease & Wellness:
Kids' Guides to Why People Get Sick and How They Can Stay Well
A KID'S GUIDE TO A HEALTHIER YOU

Village Earth Press
Vestal, NY 13850
www.villageearthpress.com

First Printing
9 8 7 6 5 4 3 2 1

Series ISBN (paperback): 978-1-62524-445-1
ISBN (paperback): 978-1-62524-413-0
ebook ISBN: 978-1-62524-048-4
   Library of Congress Control Number: 2013911241

Author: C. F. Earl.

Introduction

According to a recent study reported in the Virginia Henderson International Nursing Library, kids worry about getting sick. They worry about AIDS and cancer, about allergies and the "super-germs" that resist medication. They know about these ills—but they don't always understand what causes them or how they can be prevented.

Unfortunately, most 9- to 11-year-olds, the study found, get their information about diseases like AIDS from friends and television; only 20 percent of the children interviewed based their understanding of illness on facts they had learned at school. Too often, kids believe urban legends, schoolyard folktales, and exaggerated movie plots. Oftentimes, misinformation like this only makes their worries worse. The January 2008 *Child Health News* reported that 55 percent of all children between 9 and 13 "worry almost all the time" about illness.

This series, **Understanding Disease and Wellness**, offers readers clear information on various illnesses and conditions, as well as the immunizations that can prevent many diseases. The books dispel the myths with clearly presented facts and colorful, accurate illustrations. Better yet, these books will help kids understand not only illness—but also what they can do to stay as healthy as possible.

—*Dr. Elise Berlan*

Just the Facts

- Making sure that you stay healthy and safe is like doing a favor for yourself. It's not hard—you just have to keep a few things in mind.

- Taking care of yourself means doing things to keep yourself healthy. This includes eating a healthy diet, brushing your teeth, and getting enough sleep.

- Whenever you're playing outside, make sure you stay safe. If it's sunny outside, wear sunscreen. If it's cold, make sure to wear enough warm clothes. Headed to the pool or beach? Swim with an adult watching you and don't push anyone underwater.

- Wear a helmet when riding your bike, skateboard, or anything else with wheels.

- If you're traveling, even if it's just to the grocery store with a parent, remember to keep yourself safe. Always wear your seatbelt in the car. When taking a trip, make sure to stay close to your family and hold on to your bag.

- Stay safe at home. Make sure an adult is with you if you're cooking in the kitchen. Don't turn on the stove by yourself or use sharp knives without help. If there is ever an emergency at home, make sure you know what to do. If someone is hurt, call your local emergency number.

- If you're on the Internet, don't give out your name, address, or any other information about yourself.

- Taking care of yourself and staying safe are the best things you can do as a kid. It helps you stay ready for whatever comes next in your life. Remember—you're worth it!

Take Control!

Did You Know?

Glucose, the kind of sugar your body uses, can be found naturally in the sap of most plants and in the juice from fruit.

You might feel like people tell you what to do a lot because you're a kid. It can be tough when you feel like you don't have *control* over things around you. But you do have the power to make sure that you are the best you that you can be.

Words to Know

Control: control is the power to make decisions that change the way things are going.

You're in charge of taking care of yourself in many ways! You have to make sure you take control over doing things that keep you healthy, keep you safe, and keep you ready for whatever comes next in your life. Whether it's by wearing a helmet when riding your bike, eating foods that keep you healthy, making sure you're staying safe while enjoying your favorite sports, or wearing your seatbelt in the car, you have control over your health and safety! All you have to do is follow a few guidelines.

9

Eat the Right Foods

Eating the right foods is one of the most important ways to stay healthy. Eating right will make you feel good, and help you do well in school, sports, and other activities. Healthy foods give you the energy to keep going on a long day. And it doesn't have to be a chore—eating healthy foods is delicious.

Eating right means having a balanced *diet*. Don't eat just one sort of food all the time. Don't avoid healthy foods either.

It's best to eat lots of fruits and vegetables. Eat lots of whole grains too, like oats, brown rice, and whole-grain bread. Try to eat less junk food that has a lot of added sugar and salt. Meat, beans, and dairy can all be part of a healthy, balanced diet.

Words to Know

Diet: your diet is made up of all the food you eat, no matter what that food is.

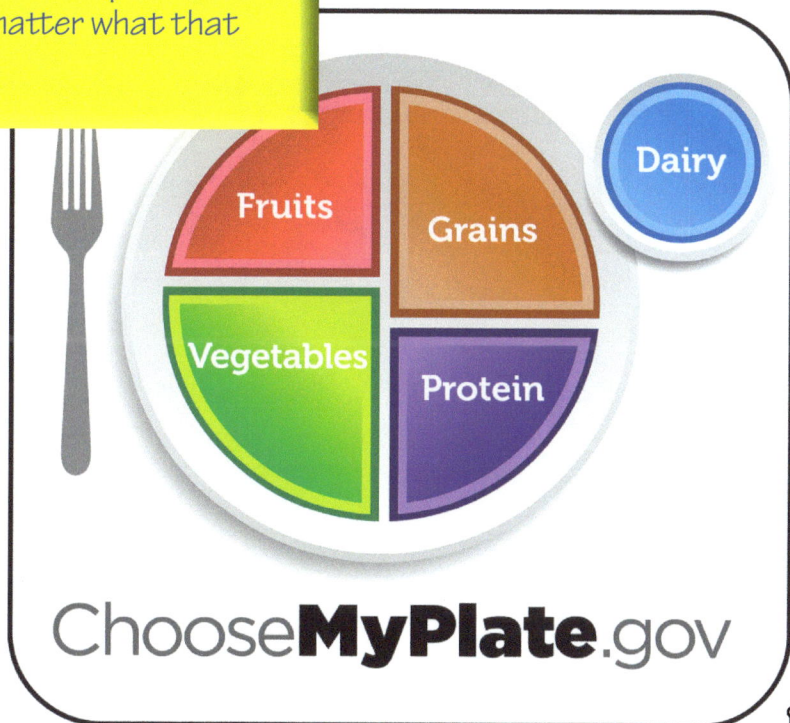

ChooseMyPlate.gov

Brush Your Teeth

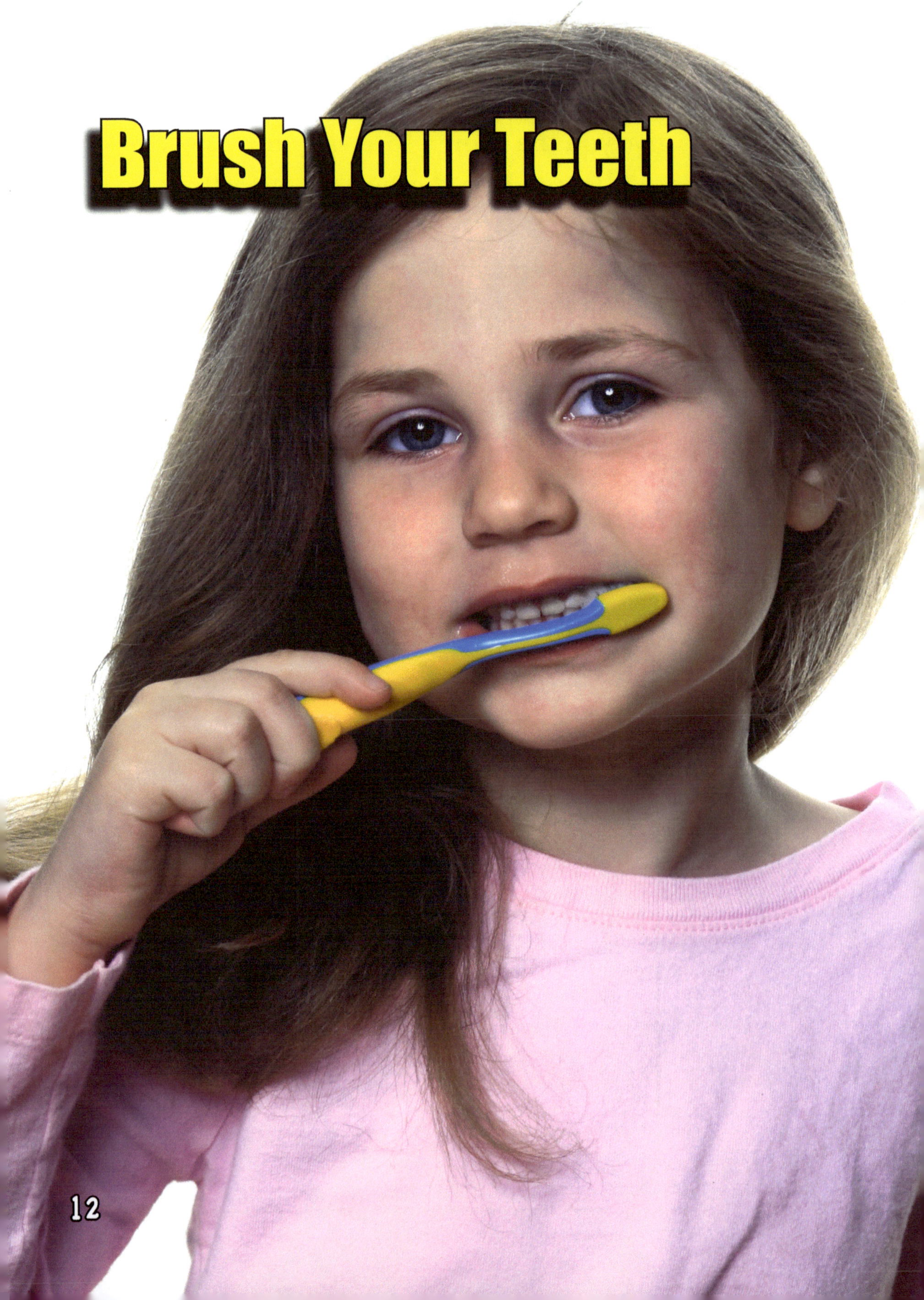

Maybe you think brushing your teeth is a chore. It's important to remember to brush, though, because it's one of the things you have control over that keeps you healthy for years to come. So how can you make sure that you're keeping your teeth and mouth healthy?

First, brush at least twice a day. Brushing more often is good, but two times per day is usually enough. Make sure you're brushing your tongue, too. Along with brushing, remember to floss every time you brush. Going to the dentist twice each year is also an important part of taking care of your teeth. Brushing and flossing can keep your teeth free of *cavities*, your gums healthy, and your breath fresh.

Words to Know

Cavities: holes or damage in the hard part of your teeth. Cavities are caused by not brushing and flossing your teeth. Cavities hurt a lot and can even lead to losing a tooth or two!

Get Plenty of Sleep

Words to Know

Active: anytime you're doing anything with your body, you're being active.

Did You Know?

No one is quite sure what happens to your brain while you sleep. Whatever is going on in there, it leaves you feeling rested and more alert. Some scientists believe that the brain sorts through information or even solves problems while you're in bed.

Think about all the things you do during the day. You go to school, hang out with friends, do homework, finish chores, and play sports, among other activities. After all that, it's time to give your body and brain a rest. Sleep recharges you for the next day. Most kids need around ten hours of sleep each night to be fully rested. Without enough sleep you might feel cranky or even have trouble thinking clearly. You may not like your bed time, but getting enough sleep will keep you happy, healthy, and *active*!

Don't Forget to Exercise

Along with eating the right foods and getting enough sleep, exercise keeps your whole body healthy. Exercises like running, playing sports, or even just playing games that require you to move around help to keep your body in shape.

Words to Know

Fit: if someone is fit, they are healthy and active.

Whenever you exercise, your body uses up the energy you take in by eating. If you eat but don't exercise, your body doesn't use up the energy. Your body ends up storing the energy in fat. You start gaining weight. So exercise keeps your weight the same and keeps you *fit*.

By exercising, you help your muscles get stronger, too. Running, swimming, riding your bike, rollerblading, and other activities all keep your muscles strong. Exercise also helps you feel happy and sleep better at night. There are lots of reasons to exercise!

Sports: Have Fun, but Play Safe

Playing sports can be a lot of fun. No matter what sport you love to play, however, it's important to make sure you're playing and practicing it safely. Injuries are common in sports, but you can reduce your risk of injury by playing safely.

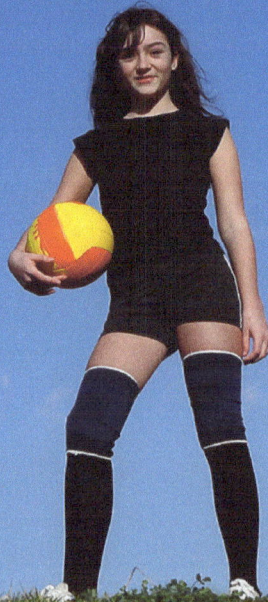

Words to Know

Equipment: in sports, pieces of equipment are the things you use to play. That might be the ball you play with as well as the pads you wear to stay safe while playing.

Each sport has its own safety rules. If you're playing a sport that's rough, you should wear the proper *equipment*, like pads and a helmet. While playing soccer, make sure to wear shin guards. Some sports might not seem dangerous, but playing by the rules will make sure no one gets hurt and everyone has fun.

Outdoor Fun

Getting outside and running around is a great way to use all your stored-up energy and to explore your world. Go outside, explore nature, and hang out with friends. There's plenty to do outdoors, whether you're playing a game, racing friends, taking a walk, or going to the park. Whenever you're heading outside to play, make sure that an adult knows where to find you. Let your parents or another adult know that you're going outside and where you're going to be.

Don't go too far away from home without taking along
a friend.

   One of the best things about all the ways kids can play
outside is that it's a way to exercise while having fun. You
might not know it, but every time you play tag, kick a soccer
ball around, or play on the monkey bars at your local park,
you're getting exercise that helps you stay healthy. Not to
mention that playing outside can be a lot of fun!

Sun

Imagine feeling the sun on your skin on a warm summer day. A sunny day is a great chance to get outside and have fun. Sometimes you're having such a good time that you forget to protect yourself from the sun. From the beach to the park, there are certain things you can do to keep on having fun and stay safe from sunburns.

Whenever you're headed outside, it's a good idea to put on some sunscreen. Sunscreen protects your skin from getting burned by the sun. Sunburns hurt a lot and put you at risk for skin cancer when you get older. Some people get sunburns more easily than others.

You need sunlight to be healthy. The sun gives you vitamin D, which helps your body function the way it should. It can even keep you feeling happy. Without vitamin D, you're more likely to get some types of diseases. So make sure to get outside and soak up some sun!

Someone with light hair and light skin burns more easily than someone with darker hair and skin, but everyone is at risk. Choose sunscreen with an SPF (Sun Protection Factor) of at least 30. The higher the SPF number, the more protection the sunscreen offers. Reapply sunscreen every so often, especially after swimming or sweating a lot.

Make sure to take breaks from being in the sun. When it's sunny and hot, you sweat, and when you sweat you lose water from your body. Drink plenty of water if you're playing outside. The sun's rays are strongest between 10:00 in the morning and 4:00 in the afternoon, so during this time make sure you're wearing sunscreen, taking breaks, and drinking lots of water.

Water

You might look forward to going to the beach or the pool all year long. When it's hot out, jumping in the water is a great way to cool off. And just as you need to stay safe while playing sports or spending time outside, it's important to stay safe while swimming or playing in the pool.

Keep the following things in mind while swimming: Always follow the rules of the pool or beach you're at. Don't go swimming without an adult around to watch you. Don't swim where it's too deep for you. Make sure to stay in the *shallow* end of the pool if you're not

Words to Know

Shallow: not very deep.

comfortable in the deep end. When playing at the pool or beach with friends, don't push anyone underwater—even if you're just playing around, you might hurt someone.

Cold

The first snowfall of winter is always a thrill, if you happen to live somewhere with cold winters. It means sledding, skating, snowballs—and cold. There are lots of ways to have fun during the winter while making sure you're safe from the cold at the same time.

First, before you go outside when the weather is cold, make sure you're wearing warm clothes. Covering up with a warm jacket, hat, and gloves can keep you from getting cold no matter what the temperature is outside. It's a good idea to wear layers of clothing, so that you can take some clothing off if you start to get too warm.

26

Wearing a warm hat is an important part of staying warm because a lot of your body heat leaves through your head. Gloves help your hands and fingers stay warm, too. Your fingers can get pretty cold if you play in the snow a lot, so make sure to wear gloves that don't let water in. That way, you can throw all the snowballs you want!

Remember to take breaks while you're playing outside in the cold weather, especially if you stop being able to feel your fingers or skin (on your face or ears, for instance). This can happen if you're playing in the cold without the proper clothing on, but it's possible even with warm clothes. Being out in extreme cold for too long can cause *frostbite* in fingers, toes, or ears. If you start to feel too cold, take a break from playing and head back inside where it's warm.

Words to Know

Frostbite: injury to the skin and the tissue underneath due to cold. Skin starts to look white and waxy, and may blister.

Hanging Out in the Neighborhood

Whenever you're exploring your neighborhood, you still have to think about staying safe. Just because you're close to home doesn't mean that safety isn't important.

When you're hanging out in your neighborhood, be careful about picking anything up off the ground, whether it's something you find in the woods or on the street. It can be hard to tell what is safe and what isn't, so it's best not to take a chance

by picking something unfamiliar up. That mushroom you found in the woods? It may look like the kind you eat with your dinner at home, but it could be dangerous. Look all you want—but don't eat it!

Whenever you go outside, make sure that your parents know where you are. Stay in areas that you know and don't stray too far, or you might not be able to find your way back.

Strangers

You might have heard your parents or other adults tell you to never talk to strangers. It's good advice you should follow. A stranger is anyone whom you don't know. Most strangers aren't bad people—some are just friends you haven't met yet. But some strangers can be dangerous. Because it's

Words to Know

Avoid: avoiding something means staying away from it.

impossible to tell a good stranger from a dangerous one, it's best to *avoid* people you don't know.

When you're outside, try to stick with at least one friend. Always make sure a parent knows where you are. Don't take anything that a stranger tries to give you, even if he or she seems nice. If a stranger offers to take you somewhere, don't go. Stay away from strangers' cars. If you think you're in danger from a stranger, it's a good idea to make noise so that others around you know you need help.

Did You Know?

Even if a stranger offers you something you really want, don't take it. If a stranger tells you he has something to show you in his car, don't go to see it.

Going Places

Traveling is exciting! Seeing new places and new things is lots of fun, and going on vacation can be a nice way to get out of your normal *routine*. When traveling, though, your surroundings are unfamiliar. Keep a few things in mind so that you can stay safe and enjoy your trip.

Before you leave, make sure to check with your parents to see that you've got everything you'll need. While traveling, make sure your

bag or backpack is always with you. You don't want to lose your bag or get it confused with someone else's.

Whenever you're in a crowded airport or sightseeing in a new place, make sure to stay close to your family or the adults you're with. Airports and *tourist* stops are often busy places with lots of people trying to get around. You'll get where you need to go if you stay within sight of your parents. Taking trips as a family can be lots of fun, but it's important to stick together to make sure no one gets lost or left behind!

33

Bike Safety

Words to Know

Injury: when you get a cut, bruise, break a bone, or get hurt in any way, you have an injury.

Riding your bike is a great way to have fun outside. It's exciting to feel the wind in your hair and on your face as you pedal down your street. You're exercising without even knowing it. But bike riding can be dangerous if you don't take the proper safety steps.

The first thing to remember before you go outside to ride your bike is to put on a helmet. Helmets protect your head from *injury* while riding your bike. You may not think you're going to crash or have an accident, but you never know for sure. Wearing a helmet is the best thing you can do to keep yourself from getting hurt if you fall off your bike. You might also want to wear knee and elbow pads, to protect yourself if you fall. Also, make sure that when you head out of the house to ride your bike, you let someone know where you're going. Staying safe keeps bike riding fun!

Other Kinds of Wheels

Wearing a helmet while riding your bike is important, but it's something to keep in mind when skateboarding, rollerblading, or riding anything with wheels too. Riding a bike, motorbike, *ATV,* skateboard, or anything else with wheels can sometimes be dangerous. Helmets, knee pads, elbow pads, and wrist guards (all shown in the images below) all offer great protection while riding any kind of *vehicle*. Wearing a helmet and pads can keep you from hurting yourself if you fall, crash, or have some type of accident. You might think you know what you're doing and that you won't get hurt, but it *can* happen, so it's best to be prepared.

Seat Belts

One of the most important things you can do to keep yourself safe is a small thing. Whenever you get into the car to go somewhere, make sure to buckle your seat belt! Seat belts keep you safe from harm if the car stops short or hits something in an accident. Even just a big bump in the road or a sudden stop can be dangerous when not wearing a seat belt. With a seat belt on, they're no big deal.

Without a seat belt, some accidents can cause you to fly forward in the car. You could end up getting really hurt. But by taking the small step of buckling up, you can prevent some of the worst injuries caused in car accidents.

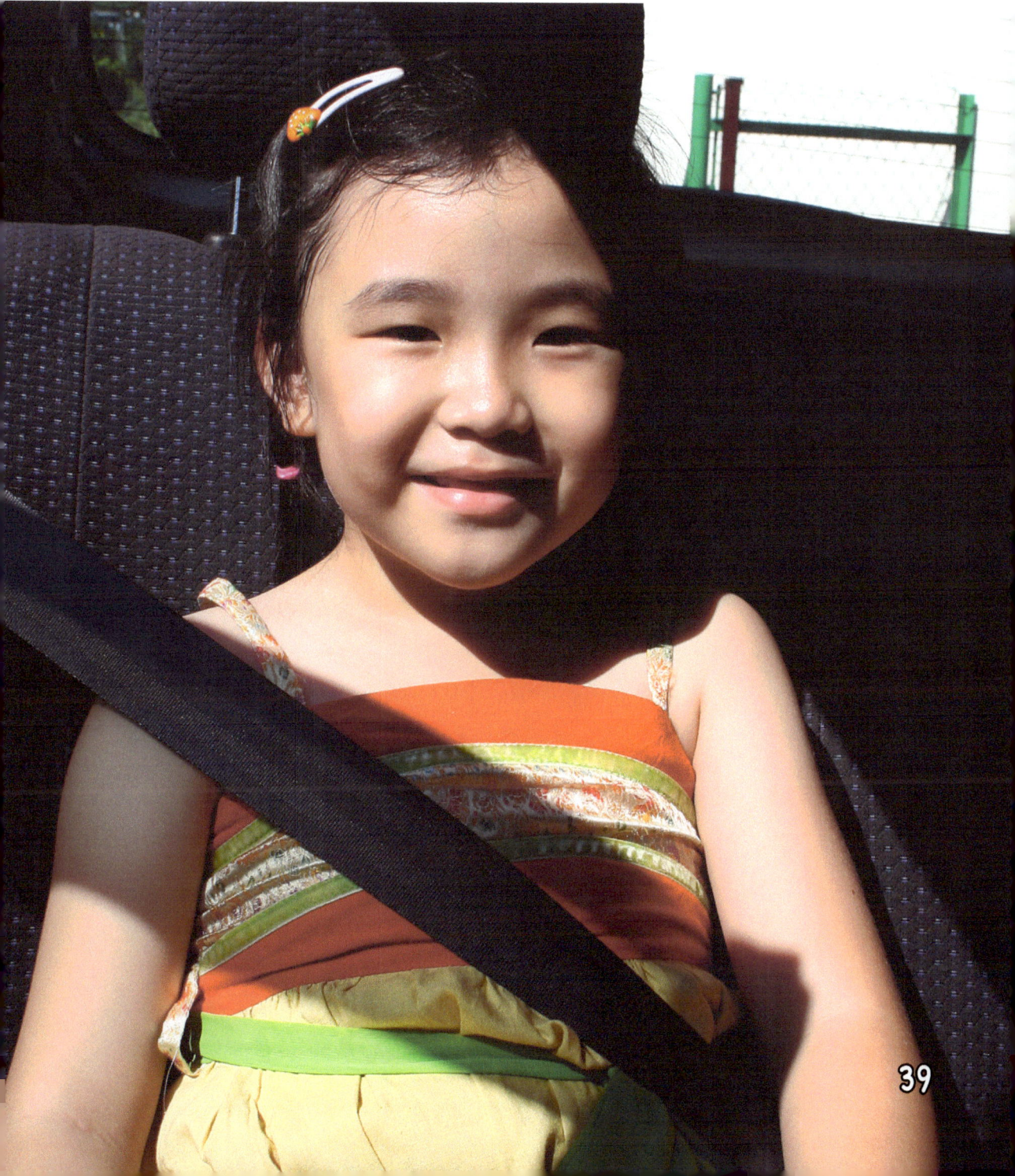

Staying Home

Did You Know?

It's important to clean up properly after cooking. That way, you can keep germs out of the kitchen. Leaving the counters and dishes dirty after cooking might seem easier, but it's best to clean up!

Your home is meant to be a safe place. And most of the time, it is. There are a few things that you should keep in mind when spending time at home, though.

If you're on the computer, make sure you understand how to stay safe on the Internet. Don't give out *personal information* like your whole name or your address online.

Being safe when you're home alone also means knowing who to call if something bad happens. Talk to your parents or guardians about an emergency phone number you should use.

There are safety steps to remember while cooking in the kitchen, too. In general, have an adult help you in the kitchen. Don't try to turn on the stove or oven without an adult around to help. When handling hot pots or pans, make sure to use oven mitts or potholders. Whenever you need to cut something, ask for help. If you're using the microwave, make sure you don't cook any metal or tinfoil in it. Finally, remember to always wash your hands before cooking!

Words to Know

Personal Information: any information that identifies you as a person. It could be your whole name, address, or phone number.

Television

Did You Know?

Ninety-nine percent of all households in the United States own at least one television. Most houses have at least two and many have three or more TVs!

Watching TV can be a great way to pass the time, learn new things, or just have fun watching your favorite shows. TV shouldn't be something that keeps you from doing other activities, though. Find a balance between watching TV and taking time to do other things. In the United States, for example, many people watch TV for around five hours a day. That's a lot when you think about all the other things a person has to do!

Make sure you're finding time for other activities like homework, playing with friends, going outside, and doing your chores. When you're sitting in front of the TV, you're not getting exercise. That's not good for your body. Make time for physical activity, and for all of the things you like to do every day!

Turn Off the TV and Your Computer

While watching TV and spending time on the computer is fun, it's important to take a break from those activities. With so much to watch on TV and so much to do online, it can be tough to pull yourself away. Spending too much time in front of the computer or TV can keep you from seeing your friends more often and getting enough exercise. It might also end up leading to health problems.

Remember, whenever you are using the Internet, it's never a good idea to give out your real name, address, or any other information about yourself. To make sure you're staying safe online, ask a parent to check on sites you want to visit first. Before signing up for any website, make sure to ask your parents if it's okay.

Home Alone

It's a big deal the first time your parents leave you home alone. It means your parents trust you, and that you're getting old enough to be *responsible* for yourself more often. But whenever you're left alone at home, you're totally in charge of keeping yourself safe.

Ask your parents if you're allowed to watch TV, go on the computer, or go outside when you're alone at home. Always know where the *emergency* numbers are. Keep any important

Words to Know

Responsible: people who are responsible can be trusted to do the right thing and take care of the things they need to.

Emergency: an emergency is a bad or dangerous situation when someone needs help.

phone numbers next to the phone so you know who to call. If something goes wrong at home, call your parents or another adult your parents trust. Call your community's emergency number if something really serious happens. If someone (including you) gets seriously hurt, or if there's a fire, call that emergency number.

Did You Know?

In lots of families, both parents work. In others, there's one parent, and he or she has to work a lot. Many kids spend some time alone after school. If you spend time alone during the day, you're one of many kids.

Fire, Accidents, and Other Emergencies

If there is ever an accident at your house, it's important to know who to call. If someone is hurt or there is a fire in the house, call your local emergency number. In Canada, the United States, and several other countries, it's 911. In the European Union, it's 112. Other countries have different numbers.

Emergency numbers put you in touch with a hospital, the police, or the fire department, depending on what kind of emergency there is at your house. After calling, help is on its way. Always remember that if there is a fire in your home, the first thing you need to do is get outside, away from the fire.

Did You Know?

Planning ahead for a fire is a great idea. You never know when there is going to be an unexpected emergency. Try practicing getting out of the house with your whole family so that you're prepared if a real fire ever happens.

Protecting Your Boundaries

Everyone has *boundaries*. These are the limits that each person has, and they are different for different people in different situations. Boundaries are like rules that each person has for how he or she wants to be treated.

One kind of boundary involves your body. Your body is yours and no one else's. No one has the right to touch you when you don't want to be touched. When you don't want to be touched, it's very important for other people to respect that. Someone might hurt you by hitting you. Or they could be hurting you by touching you in a way you don't like (touching your private parts, for instance). Either way, they shouldn't be doing it. It's not your fault, and it doesn't make you a bad person. You don't deserve to be treated that way, no matter what.

It's very important that you tell an adult you trust if someone crosses your boundary and touches you in a way

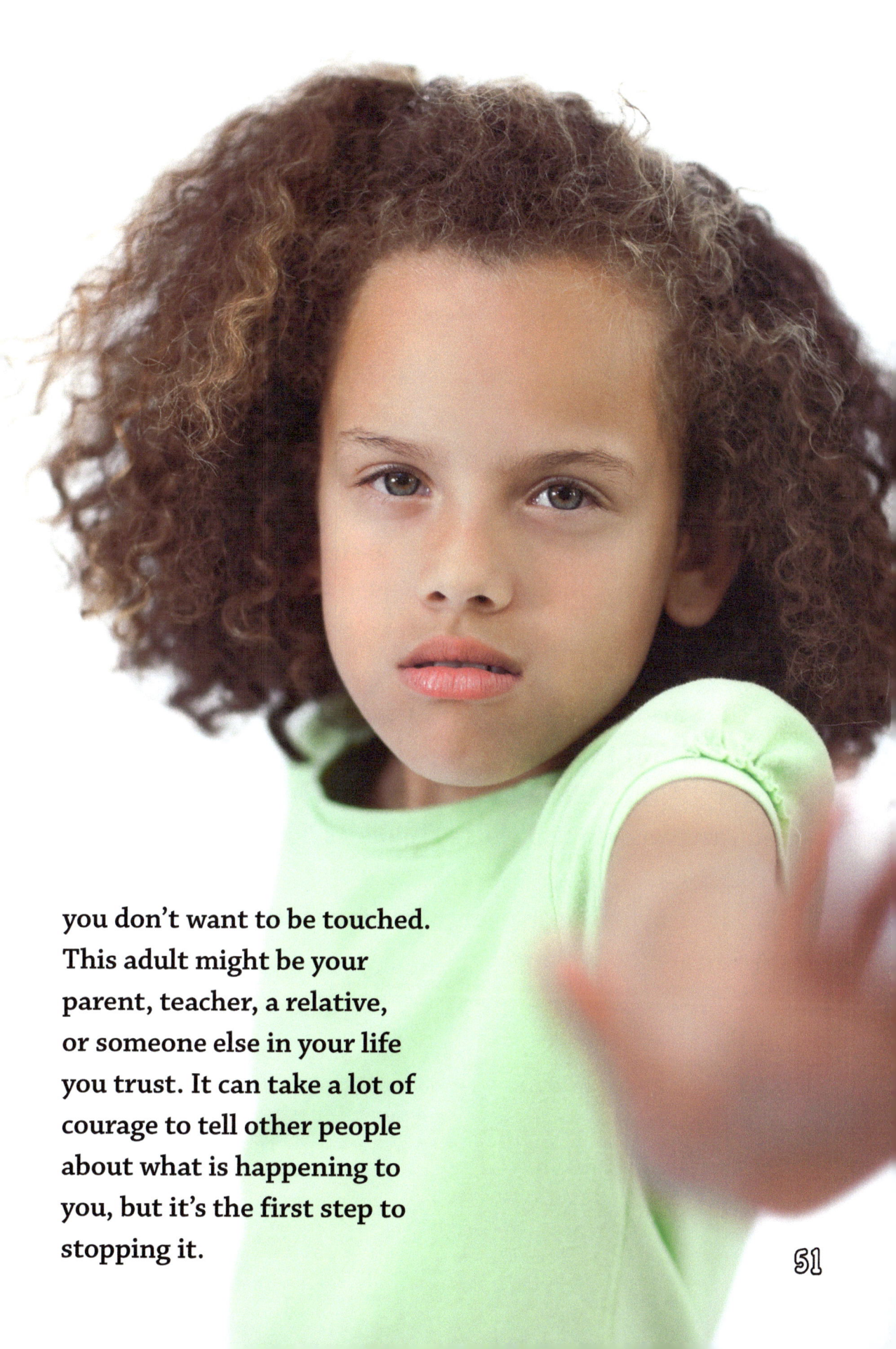

you don't want to be touched. This adult might be your parent, teacher, a relative, or someone else in your life you trust. It can take a lot of courage to tell other people about what is happening to you, but it's the first step to stopping it.

Guns

Guns aren't anything to play around with. On one hand, guns can be useful. They can be used to hunt or for sport. On the other hand, they can be weapons. They can also cause dangerous accidents. Guns aren't toys, and they aren't for kids to use without adults around. It's important to always remember that guns can be very dangerous, and even deadly. Accidents happen when guns aren't used safely and those accidents have very serious *consequences*.

If you're planning on using a gun for sport, only use it when an adult is around to *supervise*. It's never safe for a kid to be handling a gun when an adult is not around.

Never, ever point a gun at someone else.

Did You Know?

Between 40 and 45 percent of houses in the United States own guns. Most people say they own a gun to protect themselves from crime, shoot at targets, or hunt.

Consequences: consequences are the results or what happens because of something you've chosen to do.

Supervise: watching out to make sure someone does something carefully and correctly.

as a result of playing around. Kids involved in gun accidents often didn't mean to pull the trigger, or didn't mean to hit anyone when they did pulled the trigger. Often, accidents happen when we least expect it, and guns are no different.

If your family has a gun at home, it should be locked up. If you find a gun in your house, you might be tempted to pick it up. Don't do it. It's best to not touch the gun. Leave the room with the gun in it, and tell a parent that you found the gun. Keeping space between you and the gun is the best way to keep yourself safe.

If someone you know brings a gun to school or says they are going to bring a gun to school, make sure you tell a teacher as soon as you can. Guns are very serious, and it's important to take them seriously.

53

Cigarettes, Drugs, & Alcohol

Drugs are things that you put into your body to change the way it works or to change the way you feel. There are drugs that are allowed, like medicine. When you're sick, your doctor gives you medicine, which is a legal way to use drugs. Then there are drugs that are against the law. *Illegal* drugs like marijuana, cocaine, and ecstasy are often very dangerous, especially for kids. Drugs can keep you from doing well in sports and school. They can also hurt your body or mind. Even casual drug use can lead to addiction, which is when a person feels the need to use the drug all the time.

Cigarettes and alcohol are both legal drugs, but kids are not allowed to buy or use them. Your parents might drink a beer or glass of wine sometimes. Usually, that's okay. But drinking too much can hurt adults and is definitely not okay for kids. A young person's brain is still developing, and alcohol can interrupt that process. Smoking cigarettes hurts your lungs and can even cause *cancer* when you get older. To buy cigarettes and alcohol you must be a certain age. Drinking and smoking is an adult choice, and something kids should stay away from.

Words to Know

Illegal: against the law.

Cancer: cancer is made up of cells that won't stop growing. Cancer can be deadly.

Bullies

You might have heard this phrase before: "treat others in the way you want to be treated." Being kind to others is an important part of making sure everyone is the best person they can be.

Sometimes, we don't all follow that rule and people are mean to each other. Hurting or teasing another person on purpose is called bullying. Around three-quarters of kids have been picked on or bullied. That's a lot of kids! A bully can make you scared to go to school or to go outside. Bullying is very serious, and can even be dangerous if the bully goes too far.

So what can you do if you or someone you know is being bullied? There are many ways to deal with bullying. Start by telling the bully to stop picking on you. If that doesn't work, try to *ignore* the bully. By ignoring the bully, you take away some of his or her power to make you feel bad. Don't let a bully make you feel bad about who you are. You're an amazing person—you shouldn't let a bully make you feel like anything less. Try hanging out with a friend or two to take your mind off the bully. If nothing works, or a bully hurts you, make sure to tell an adult you trust.

Words to Know

Ignore: to ignore something is to not pay attention to it on purpose.

You're Worth It!

All of this health and safety advice might seem like a lot to take in. There are lots of rules, which might seem to get in the way of having fun.

But taking care of yourself by being safe and staying healthy is the most important thing you can do. Eating right, getting exercise, and taking other steps aren't just things that adults tell you to do because they want to annoy you. These things really will keep you healthier and safer so that you can keep on living your life to your full potential.

By doing stuff like wearing helmets and knowing emergency numbers, you are taking control over your own life in a very *mature* way. As you get older, you get more responsibilities. Some of those responsibilities include taking care of yourself in more and more ways.

Mature: to be mature means to be grown up.

Always remember that you have a lot to offer the rest of the world. But to do your best, you have to keep yourself healthy and safe. When you're healthier, you feel better, and feeling better allows you to do your best.

So take control. You're worth the effort! Take care of yourself so that you can do the things you want to. Think about it: you can't reach your dreams if you're not healthy, happy, and safe.

59

Find Out More

Children's Health International
childrenshealthintl.org

D.A.R.E. - Drug Abuse Resistance Education
www.dare.com

Health and Fitness - Fitness and Exercise
www.kids.gov/k_5/k_5_health_issues.shtml

Kids Health
www.kidshealth.org

Nutrition for Kids
nutritionforkids.com

PBS Kids Go!: Its My Life. Friends. Bullies.
pbskids.org/itsmylife/friends/bullies

Safe Kids
www.safekids.org/worldwide

Sun Safety
www.sunsafetyforkids.org

Index

Picture Credits

Dreamstime.com:

8: Andres Rodriguez

9: Dreamstime.com Agency

10: Nagy-bagoly Ilona

12: Anita Patterson Peppers

13: Gavril Bernad

14: Xiebiyun

17: Spotmatik

18-19: Godfer

20: Mirmoor

21: Sonya Etchison

22: Jennifer Badeaux

23: Bigandt

24: Varina And Jay Patel

25 left: Robert Adrian Hillman

25 right: Nickondr

26: Mykhaylo Palinchak

27: Prairierattler

28: Beata Becla

29 top: Saša Prudkov

29 bottom: Pavel Losevsky

30: Madartists

31: Photoeuphoria

32: Nyul

33: Okea

34: Pro777

35: Paolo Pagani

36 left: Anatoliy Samara

36 right: Brad Sauter

37 left: Refat Mamutov

37 right: Vvksam

38: Sonya Etchison

39: Goh Siok hian

40: Sashkinw

42: Wavebreakmedia Ltd

43: Ejwhite

44: Grzegorzmoment

45: Ronnie Patrick

46: Stefano Lunardi

47: Shime

48-49: Crystal Craig

50: Fernando Jose Vascocelos Soares

51: Wavebreakmedia Ltd

52-53: Fabinus08

54: Maxim Shebeko

55: Mark Rasmussen

56: Vuk Vukmirovic

57: Marcel De Grijs

58: Aliona Zbughin

59: Manav Lohia

11: USDA | ChooseMyPlate.gov

To the best knowledge of the publisher, all other images are in the public domain. If any image has been inadvertently uncredited, please notify Village Earth Press, Vestal, New York 13850, so that rectification can be made for future printings.

About the Author

C. F. Earl has written many books for young adults and children. He lives in New York State in the United States.

About the Consultant

Elise DeVore Berlan, MD, MPH, FAAP, is a faculty member of the Division of Adolescent Health at Nationwide Children's Hospital and an Assistant Professor of Clinical Pediatrics at the Ohio State University College of Medicine. She completed her fellowship in adolescent medicine at Children's Hospital Boston and obtained a master's degree in public health at the Harvard School of Public Health. Dr. Berlan completed her residency in pediatrics at the Children's Hospital of Philadelphia, where she also served an additional year as chief resident. She received her medical degree from the University of Iowa College of Medicine.

www.ingramcontent.com/pod-product-compliance
Lightning Source LLC
Chambersburg PA
CBHW042017080426

42735CB00002B/86